Yellow Umbrella Books are published by Capstone Press
151 Good Counsel Drive, P.O. Box 669, Mankato, Minnesota 56002
http://www.capstone-press.com

Library of Congress Cataloging-in-Publication Data
Trumbauer, Lisa, 1963-
  Who need plants? / by Lisa Trumbauer.
    p. cm.
    Includes Index.
  Summary: Explores some of the ways that animals and people use plants for food and shelter.
  ISBN 0-7368-2023-X (Hardcover)
  1. Plants–Miscellanea–Juvenile literature. [1. Plants--Miscellanea.] I. Title.
  QK49.T77 2003
  581.6'3–dc21

                                                                    2003000611

Editorial Credits

Mary Lindeen, Editorial Director; Jennifer Van Voorst, Editor; Wanda Winch, Photo Researcher

Photo Credits

Cover: Corbis; Title Page: Photo 24/Brand X Pictures; Page 2: PhotoLink/PhotoDisc; Page 3: Stockbyte; Page 4: Photo 24/Brand X Pictures; Page 5: Lynn and Donna Rogers; Page 6: Photo 24/Brand X Pictures; Page 7: Trevor Lindegger/Image Ideas, Inc.; Page 8: David Buffington/PhotoDisc; Page 9: Mark Karrass/Corbis; Page 10: Mark Andersen/RubberBall Productions; Page 11: Image Source/elektraVision; Page 12: Ron Chapple/Thinkstock; Page 13: Keith Weller/USDA/ARS; Page 14: Erin Hogan/PhotoDisc; Page 15: Photo 24/Brand X Pictures; Page 16: John Wong/RubberBall Productions

Who Needs Plants?

By Lisa Trumbauer

Consultant: Patrice Morrow, Ph.D., Professor, Department of Ecology, Evolution, and Behavior, University of Minnesota, Twin Cities

Yellow Umbrella Books

an imprint of Capstone Press
Mankato, Minnesota

Rabbits live in bushes.

Birds live in trees. Animals need plants for shelter.

Deer like to eat leaves.

Bears like to eat berries.
Animals need plants for food.

Monkeys rest in the shade of the forest.

Lions rest in the shade of a tree. Animals need plants for shade.

People need plants, too.
People use trees to
build houses.

Houses give us shelter.

People need plants for shade.

Shade keeps people cool.

People need plants for food.

Fruits and vegetables are plants people eat.

What else needs plants?

The Earth needs plants.

Plants make the Earth beautiful.

Words to Know/Index

Word Count: 97
Early-Intervention Level: 8